CW00557266

5

Knowledge about Language

Written by

M.M. Firth and A.G. Ralston

Illustrations by

O.R. Davison

ISBN 0 7169 6007 9

© M.M Firth & A.G. Ralston, 1996.

The authors would like to acknowledge with thanks the contribution of Mr. Alec Dunlop, Principal Teacher of English at Hutchesons' Grammar School, Glasgow, in providing the original idea for this book.

ROBERT GIBSON · Publisher
17 Fitzroy Place, Glasgow, G3 7SF, Scotland, U.K.

Contents

COPYING PROHIBITED

Note: This publication is NOT licensed for copying under the Copyright Licensing Agency's Scheme, to which Robert Gibson & Sons are not party.

All rights reserved. No part of this publication may be reproduced; stored in a retrieval system; or transmitted in any form or by any means – electronic, mechanical, photocopying, or otherwise – without prior permission of the publisher Robert Gibson & Sons, Ltd., 17 Fitzroy Place, Glasgow, G3
Printed by Bell and Bain Ltd., Glasgow

Introduction for Teachers

'Knowledge about language' is one of the key aspects of the 5 - 14 English language programme. The 1991 Scottish Office Education Department document *English Language 5 - 14* stresses that children should acquire knowledge of 'a selection of the terms referring to the words, grammar and sounds of the language... Such knowledge should support and supplement the continuing, natural processes of language acquisition' (page 7). A similar thrust is apparent in the Department for Education's *English in the National Curriculum*, which refers to the need for children to recognise that 'standard English is distinguished from other forms of English by its vocabulary, and by rules and conventions of grammar, spelling and punctuation.'

Obviously, this has always been a major component of English teaching. In the past, however, the teaching of language and grammar has sometimes been approached in a rigid and mechanical way, with areas such as parsing and general analysis being taught purely for their own sake and no attempt being made to show their relevance to the 'real' use of language in everyday speaking, listening, reading and writing.

At the same time, many teachers feel that the pendulum has swung too far in the opposite direction. Indeed, younger teachers are likely to have come through an education system in which language and grammar were tackled in the most perfunctory way, if at all. Such teachers may even find themselves having to learn for the first time some of the basic terminology of parts of speech and sentence analysis which is indispensable for the 5-14 writing programme attainment outcomes and for the teaching of English at Key Stages 2 and 3. Knowledge of linguistic and grammatical terminology is, moreover, vital for Higher and 'A' Level English. Teachers who, like the authors of the present volume, have had experience both of presenting candidates and of assessing scripts for the various Examination Boards will be particularly aware that interpretation questions such as 'comment on the sentence structure' are very badly handled by the majority of candidates who simply lack knowledge of the necessary terminology with which to express their answers.

Every English teacher, of course, will have tattered copies of long out of print textbooks to which he or she can refer back for this information. We nevertheless felt that a presentation of what might be called 'the basics' in an updated format would be of assistance to teachers involved with pupils in the early years of secondary school.

'With regular practice,' says the 5 - 14 report, 'the pupil should be taught to give increasing priority to technical features and presentation of the text through control of sentence structure, punctuation, spelling and handwriting.' By Level E, pupils are expected to recognise terms such as noun, verb, adjective, adverb, pronoun, conjunction, paragraph, singular, plural, subject, predicate, clause, topic sentence and so on. All these key terms – and many others – are covered in this book.

The teacher will naturally use his or her judgment as to how far the study of a particular topic should be pursued. In most cases there are sufficient exercises provided to allow abler pupils to work ahead if necessary. Attention has also been given to structuring the book in a logical and progressive way, but the material is quite suitable for the teacher to deal with in any order. At the end of each section, the 'Progress Report' box summarises what has been covered so far and an Appendix has been provided at the end of the whole book, listing all the language terms used in connection with 5-14 and the National Curriculum Key Stages 2 and 3 and relating these to the appropriate pages where exercises can be found. This will enable teachers to check that no important aspect of the Writing programme has been omitted from their course of lessons.

There has always been much controversy about what is 'right' and 'wrong' in grammar and as language is constantly changing it is obviously foolish to be dogmatic and prescriptive. We have tried to describe the usage that is currently considered generally acceptable by educated people and we occasionally point out where 'rules' appear to be changing as a form previously deemed unacceptable is becoming widespread.

Introduction for Pupils

Do we *have* to study grammar?

We all need to be able to communicate with other people, by talking, listening, writing and reading. Grammar is simply a study of how we put words together into sentences that others can understand. There has to be an agreed way of doing this – otherwise we would all be constantly misunderstood.

This book will explain to you what the main types of words are called and show you how groups of words can be put together to form phrases, clauses, sentences and paragraphs.

Teachers are sometimes asked, "Do we really need to know all these terms like adjectives, verbs, participles, subordinate clauses and so on?"

These technical names are used simply to help explain how words work. It is obviously simpler for a motorist to go to his garage and ask for a new exhaust by name, rather than saying that he needs a long metal pipe to take away the gases emitted by the engine of the car.

In the same way, knowing the precise names for different aspects of the English language will help you to understand much better how the language works. For instance, if you sometimes have difficulty understanding what a sentence is, knowledge of terms like subject, verb and object will help to make this clearer.

Grammar does not have to be dull and mechanical! We have tried to make the exercises more interesting by using pictures and word games.

When you see a box headed

O   O   O   O   O   O   O   O   O   O

memo:

this will remind you of an important rule to remember when doing the exercise which follows.

At the end of each section of the book a box headed

Progress Report

will sum up all the topics covered in that section, to help you check how you are gradually adding to your knowledge about language.

Part One
Types of Word

1.   NOUNS

What is a noun?

Exercise 1

Horace, the cat, spends most of his time snoozing on top of the television, but he likes to imagine he is a hero. Here, he is imagining he is a war reporter on a dangerous mission. The paragraph below tells the story of the cartoon strip, but some words have been omitted. Copy the paragraph into your jotter and fill in the blanks with single words. You will find most of them in this introduction or in the cartoon 'bubbles'.

.... is lying on top of the ...., listening to the news. He hears that enemy .... have just made a .... In Horace's fantasy, he is called on by the *Daily Whisker* as a war .... He grabs his .... and dashes to the .... to catch the midnight .... He imagines the admiring .... of the other .... and the flight .... He can hear them praising his .... and .... Then he pictures a newspaper .... saying an ace reporter has been wounded in .... Horace realises this .... might be fatal! He abandons his .... and goes back to sleep.

The words you have filled in are all **nouns.** It can be useful to think of nouns as <u>naming</u> words. A noun is a word used to refer to a person, a place or a thing.

Exercise 2

Look around the classroom. Write down ten nouns which name things you can see. These could include names of objects, such as 'book', names of people, such as 'Susan', and even the names of ideas like 'concentration' – or 'boredom'!

Exercise 3

This extract is adapted from a book you may have read, called *Matilda* by Roald Dahl. It is about a girl who is very intelligent and has special powers. This paragraph describes Matilda at school. There are 13 nouns in it. Make a list of them in your jotter.

Matilda displayed almost no signs of her brilliance and she never showed off. Unless you started a discussion with her about literature or mathematics, you would never have known the extent of her brain-power. All those in her class liked her. And they knew also that she was allowed to sit quietly with a book during lessons and not pay attention to the teacher.

o   o   o   o   o   o   o   o   o   o   o

memo:

There are four kinds of noun :
Common *(things) :* cat, girl.
Proper *(special things) :* Horace. *(Proper nouns have a*
capital letter.)
Collective *(groups of things) :* crew.
Abstract *(ideas; feelings) :* flair; mission.

Exercise 4

(a) Put the following nouns into the correct column :

Edinburgh	camera	discussion	set
troop	Matilda	button	class
fear	herd	James	courage
book	imagination	Germany	aeroplane

Common	Proper	Collective	Abstract

More difficult!

(b) Think of another two nouns of each type and add them to your lists. Exchange your list with a partner, and discuss your additions. Decide if they have been put into the correct box.

(c) Pick one or more noun from each list and draw them.

Discuss: ❑ Which type of noun was easy to draw? Why?

❑ Which nouns would be hardest to draw? Why?

Singular or Plural?

When there is only one of something, it is said to be **singular**.

 bird

When there is more than one, it is said to be **plural**.

birds

Forming plurals.

Nouns form plurals in several different ways. Although there are general rules, there are many exceptions. Always check with a dictionary. The next exercise will help you understand some of the ways plurals are formed in English.

Exercise 5

(a) Fill in the plurals of the following nouns, using a dictionary to check, if necessary. The first one is done for you.

1. boy	boys	7. foot	
2. glass		8. shelf	
3. child		9. chief	
4. fly		10. deer	
5. hero		11. cactus	
6. piano		12. eye-witness	

(b) With a group or partner, look back at how you formed the plurals in the 12 examples above. Write down brief rules to explain how you formed the plurals in different ways. For example : Example 1 : word + s. In numbers 5 and 6 and numbers 8 and 9, the last letter in the original word is important.

Your rule might begin, "If words end in 'o', . . ."

(c) Think of one or two more examples of each type.

Collective Nouns

It has become the custom to use particular collective nouns for certain things. A group of cows is a **herd**, while a group of sheep is a **flock**. Some collective nouns are specifically used for one thing only : a **pride** of lions.

Exercise 6

Can you place the following words correctly in the spaces?

gang; locusts; ships; litter; shoal; flowers; gaggle; swarm; pack; herd.

A .... of fish	A .... of thieves
A .... of wolves	A plague of ....
A fleet of	A .... of bees
A ....of elephants	A .... of kittens
A bunch of	A .... of geese

A **class** of children

Exercise 7

In pairs or groups, think of as many more 'collections' as you can.

More difficult!

❑   The poet Laurie Lee invented a collective noun of his own: a <u>dignity</u> of grandmothers. (What kind of noun is 'dignity' usually?) Discuss why this was a good choice of word.

❑   Can you invent some new collective nouns? You could try to think of a suitable one for the following groups: babies; cars; shoppers; boys; tourists.

Write it out like this: a .... of ....

Fewer or Less?

Some nouns refer to things which can be individually counted: cat; book.

Others refer to things which occur in a mass and cannot be counted individually: ice; water; friendliness.

0   0   0   0   0   0   0   0   0   0   0

memo:

The word 'less' should not be used with nouns which can be counted; 'fewer' should always be used instead. 'Less' should only be used with nouns which cannot be individually counted.

Exercise 8

Put 'fewer' or 'less' into the blanks as appropriate :

1.   There are .... apples than there were last autumn.
2.   In our class there are .... girls than boys.
3.   .... people go to the theatre than go to the cinema.
4.   There will be .... snow in future as a result of global warming.
5.   There are .... small birds since the spread of magpies.

When is a noun not a noun?

You should remember, though, that words can perform different jobs in a sentence. For example, the word 'orange' is only a noun when it is used to mean the name of the fruit.

Exercise 9

In the following pairs of sentences the underlined words are used once as a noun, and once as something else. Pick out the examples which are nouns.

1.   *(a)*   At break I ate an <u>orange</u>.
         (b)   The chair had an <u>orange</u> cushion.

2.   *(a)*   If it docs not rain I shall <u>water</u> the garden.
         (b)   <u>Water</u> poured through the leaky roof.

3.   *(a)*   Horace is skating on the <u>ice</u>.
         (b)   I will <u>ice</u> the cake with pink icing

4.   *(a)*   There was a green <u>light</u> on the dock.
         (b)   The curtains were <u>light</u> green.

5.   *(a)*   Liverpool F.C. built a new <u>stand</u>.
         (b)   As the train was full we had to <u>stand</u>.

2.   VERBS

Is a verb a 'doing' word?

This is quite a useful definition, as a verb is generally a word which refers to an action. 'Swim', 'speak', 'run' and 'fly' are examples. However, although verbs usually refer to things that we 'do', you must remember that words like 'be', 'become' and 'have' are also verbs. Such words refer to states, rather than actions. The work of verbs in the sentence is to say what the subject of the sentence <u>is</u> or <u>does</u>. By adding endings or extra parts, a verb can also indicate the time of the action or state – this is known as the 'tense' of the verb and is explained on page 19.

Exercise 10

Look around the classroom and out of the window if you have a good view. Your teacher will give you one minute to make a list of verbs which express actions you can see people doing :

For example, **write**.

Score a point for each verb you have written within the minute.

Exercise 11

The Pied Piper by Robert Browning is a poem which tells the story of a plague of rats which are magically charmed away by a man playing on a pipe. When the poet is describing the invasion of the rats he uses many verbs to create a sense of bustling action.

In the following extract the verbs have been omitted and are listed below. In groups, discuss which verb you think best fits in each space and fill them in. Afterwards you can compare your version with Browning's original text.

Rats!
They .... the dogs, and .... the cats,
   And .... the babies in the cradles,
And .... the cheeses out of the vats,
   And .... the soup from the cooks' own ladles,
.... open the kegs of salted sprats,
............nests inside men's Sunday hats,
And even .... the women's chats
     By .... their ....
     With .... and ....
In fifty different sharps and flats.

shrieking	licked	fought	squeaking
split	speaking	ate	killed
made	spoiled	drowning	bit

Is it a verb?

Do you remember that, when we looked at nouns, we discovered the same word could do different jobs in a sentence?

Exercise 12

In the following pairs of sentences, the underlined word is used once as a noun and once as a verb. With a partner, discuss the two sentences and pick out the sentence in which the word is used as a verb.

1. *(a)* Compass needles <u>point</u> north.
   (b) The pencil had a sharp <u>point</u>.

2. *(a)* <u>Love</u> is blind.
   (b) I <u>love</u> chocolate.

3. *(a)* I <u>spy</u> with my little eye.
   (b) The <u>spy</u> carried a hidden camera.

4. *(a)* The wizard <u>cast</u> a spell.
   (b) The play had a large <u>cast</u>.

5. *(a)* Birds of a feather <u>flock</u> together.
   (b) A <u>flock</u> of sheep was blocking the road.

Taking verbs apart

It is not possible to understand how a car engine works without taking it apart, and it is the same with verbs. It is also necessary to learn the names of a few main parts. Although this may seem unnecessary, it is the best way to understand in the long run.

A verb consists of a **stem** (main part) and a **suffix** ('s', 'es', 'ed', 'ing').

> walked = walk + ed

The 'stem' gives the basic meaning of the action; the 'suffix' is an ending which gives some extra information such as when the action took place, or whether it was done by one person or more than one.

Three special forms of the verb

In order to discuss how writers use language, it is useful to know some technical terms. There are three special verb forms which you should learn to recognise.

❑   1.   The **infinitive**.

This is formed by the word 'to' + the verb stem.

Example :

He began to speak.

❑   2.   The **present participle**.

This is formed by adding 'ing' to the stem. Forms ending with 'ing' can be part of the main verb :

Fish were swimming in the lake.

They can also do the work of nouns and adjectives :

Swimming is good for you. The speaking clock.

❑ 3. The **past participle**.

This is formed by adding a suffix (usually 'ed') to the stem or by changing the sound of the stem. The past participle is used in forms of the past tense with 'have' and 'had':

I have <u>broken</u> the vase.

Susie had <u>baked</u> a cake.

It can also be used as an adjective:

a <u>broken</u> vase; a <u>baked</u> potato.

Both types of participle can be used as linking words to join two sentences together. This is explained in Part II of this book.

Exercise 13

Can you identify the 2 infinitives, 2 present participles and 2 past participles in the following sentence?

I was beginning to learn the language after a month in Germany, but I was finding the written language harder to understand than the spoken word.

(a)   The infinitives are.................... and ....

(b)   The present participles are .... and ....

(c)   The past participles are.......................... and ....

The 'split infinitive'

"To boldly go, where no man has gone before...."

Do you remember these famous words from the opening of *Star Trek*?

It is generally agreed that no other word should come between the two words of the infinitive as happens in 'to boldly go'. This is known as a **split infinitive** and, although you may see it frequently in print, many people consider it bad style and it is therefore better to avoid it.

Exercise 14

In this extract from *The Pied Piper*, Browning uses a great many present participles. At this point in the story, the pied piper, who has been cheated of the money promised him for disposing of the rats, plays a different tune which attracts all the children. Write down the present participles and then, with a partner, discuss the effect of the use of them.

There was a rustling, that seemed like a bustling
Of merry crowd justling at pitching and hustling,
Small feet were pattering, wooden shoes clattering,
Little hands clapping and little tongues chattering,
And, like fowls in a farm-yard when barley is scattering,
Out came the children running.

O   O   O   O   O   O   O

memo:

Infinitives and participles cannot do the job of a main verb in a sentence.

What is the time?

In English, the form of the verb will tell you **when** the action took place. This is known as '**tense**'. The clue will be found in the ending of the verb or in an alteration to the sound of it (for example from 'speak' to 'spoke'), or in the use of some extra words like 'shall' or 'had'.

The extra words such as 'shall', 'will', 'have been', are known as **auxiliaries**. These may be separated from the main verb by other words :

   He <u>will</u> soon <u>be coming</u> home.

   <u>Will</u> you <u>take</u> the job?

Here are some examples of different tenses. All parts of the verb are underlined for you.

Past: The rats <u>ate</u> the food. The piper <u>had heard</u> of the
               problem.
Present: I <u>walk</u> to school. Horace <u>is watching</u> television.
Future: I <u>shall drive</u> to school tomorrow.

Exercise 15

Jim was a new apprentice at Harry's Motors. He was given the job of removing all the parts of the verbs from these sentences. Write them out for him in the spaces provided.

1 The rats were biting the babies in the cradles.
2. I am living in a top floor flat.
3. I shall speak to you again tomorrow.
4. The mirror cracked from side to side.
5. I have not seen her for many years.

1.	2.	3.	4.	5.

Now, decide whether the five verbs are in the present, past or future tense :

1.	2.	3.	4.	5.

Past tense or past participle?

Some verbs form their past tense and past participle by adding 'ed':

walk / walked;

Others do so by changing the stem vowel:

swim / swam / swum.

❑ Sometimes, but not always, the vowels in the past tense and the past participle may be different. For example, 'swam' is past tense; 'swum' is the past participle. A common error is to use the participle form where the past tense is required.

Exercise 16

Copy the following table and complete it according to the pattern of the first example, filling in the missing forms of the verb. (Remember that the past participle is the form that is used after 'have', 'has' or 'had'.)

Present Tense	Past Tense	Past Participle
drink	drank	(has) drunk
throw		
see		
buy		
	went	
		(has) rung
do		

Exercise 17

Rewrite these sentences, changing the verbs to **past** tense.

1. Claire chooses her own clothes.
2. The police are looking into the matter.
3. The group sing a mixture of rock and pop.
4. I feed my mother's dog.
5. They are all in the football team.

Shall or will?

```
O  O  O  O  O  O  O  O

memo:

Use :

'Shall' after 'I' or 'we'.
'Will' after  'you'; 'he', 'she' or 'it'; and 'they'.
```

Exercise 18

Rewrite the sentences in Exercise 17, this time changing the verbs to future tense.

Story writing.

In English, most story writing is in the past tense, although sometimes the present is used to create special effects. A common error in writing is to switch tenses accidentally while telling a story.

Exercise 19

(a)   Discuss the following examples with your partner. Mark with a line where the verbs suddenly change from present to past tense.

(b)   Rewrite each paragraph, using either present or past tense only.

1.   My alarm clock rings loudly. Monday morning. The worst day in the week. Reluctantly I get out of bed, get dressed and go downstairs. My sister was in the kitchen having breakfast. I asked her if she could lend me some money for the bus fare. She laughed.

2.   The beach is crowded with people on this sunny Saturday afternoon. Children are digging with buckets and spades and some are paddling in the water, screaming and splashing. Suddenly I noticed someone waving from an air-bed which had drifted out to sea. No one else seemed to have seen it, so I raced over to the life-guard's chair. He had gone!

Do the numbers agree?

This sentence was written by a Higher English candidate in an exam. What is wrong with the sentence?

> *One in ten people are overweight.*

This is a very common error. The subject of the sentence, 'one', is singular, but the verb, 'are', is plural. The subject of a sentence **must always** agree with its verb in number. If the subject is singular then the verb must be singular. Similarly, a plural subject takes a plural verb.

---

0   0   0   0   0   0   0   0   0   0   0   0

memo:

The following words are **always** *followed by a singular verb:*

one	each	none	neither

Two more points to note:

❑   1.   'There <u>was</u>' is followed by the singular; 'There <u>were</u>' must be used before plurals :

There **was** a dog in the room.

BUT

There **were** hundreds of people at the meeting.

❑   2.   Collective nouns are usually followed by a singular verb, but the plural is optional, especially if the group is one of people or if individual members of the group are focused upon.

ST GEORGE'S SCHOOL
FOR GIRLS

– ENGLISH DEPT –

Exercise 20

Copy these sentences, using the correct form of the verb :

1. One in three people (wear / wears) glasses.
2. None of us (was / were) interested in going on the school trip.
3. My class (like / likes) our new teacher.
4. There (was / were) hundreds of homeless people sleeping in doorways.
5. Each of us (has / have) a copy of the book.
6. There (was / were) four people in the room.
7. Each of us (has / have) passed the exam.
8. Neither of the tennis players (was / were) in top form.
9. A swarm of bees (is / are) supposed to be lucky.
10. Neither of us (is / are) going to the party.

Now compare your answers with a partner and decide if your verbs all agree in number with the subjects of the sentences. Which sentence has two possible correct answers? (Clue : see Note 2 on previous page.)

Commands

A verb may be used to give a command.

Shut the door! Give me the book.

The part of the verb used is the infinitive without 'to'. This form is sometimes known as the **imperative**.

Commands are frequently used in the language of advertising and when the tone of writing is persuasive. They are also used in instructions, such as recipes.

Exercise 21

Pick out the imperative verbs (commands) in the following recipe.

To make tablet, put 1 lb. sugar in a large, thick saucepan, adding 1/4 pint single cream and a pinch of salt. Heat over a low gas, stirring steadily until the sugar has melted. Then raise the heat to moderate, cease stirring and let it boil steadily until it reaches 118 °C. Remove pan from the heat and beat mixture well. When the bubbles have stopped forming, stir in 1/4 teaspoon of vanilla essence and continue to beat till it thickens. Tip into a greased tin and leave to cool.

Active or passive?

Again, these are technical terms which are useful in discussing how language is used.

When the subject of the verb is actually performing the action, the verb is said to be **active** or **in the active voice**. When the subject is having the action done to it, the verb is said to be **passive** or **in the passive voice**.

Basically, the sentence means the same, but the emphasis is altered, as more stress is placed on the subject of the sentence.

Active: The dog snatched the bone	Passive: The bone was snatched by the dog

It is useful to be able to distinguish these forms as writers use them deliberately to achieve certain effects. Formal, impersonal writing, as in reports, legal documents or scientific writing, often makes use of the passive.

Formula for changing an active verb to passive:

1. *Exchange positions of subject and object in the sentence.*
2. *Replace the verb by the appropriate part of 'to be' + past participle.*
3. *Insert the preposition 'by' before the former subject.*

Exercise 22

Change the following sentences from active to passive:

1.   The traveller told a thrilling story.
2.   Lorries bring the goods.
3.   Electricity lights our homes.
4.   A chauffeur brought him to work.
5.   A falling tree crushed the car.

Exercise 23

Change the following sentences from passive to active.

1.   The top prize was won by the head girl.
2.   He has been left a fortune by his grandfather.
3.   'The Last Supper' was painted by Leonardo.
4.   My rabbit was killed by a fox.
5.   John was always being bullied by Steven.

3.   ADJECTIVES

An adjective is a 'describing' word.

❑   An adjective adds more information to a noun. Adjectives help a
     reader to have a clearer picture or understanding of the thing
     being written about.

Horace has <u>pointed</u> ears

A dodo had a <u>large</u> beak

Exercise 24

What am I?

Write down six adjectives which you would most like to hear used in a description of yourself. Then write six you would hate to hear. Compare your list with others in the class. Are the words you have written down all adjectives?

Exercise 25

You should generally be careful not to overdo the use of adjectives in your writing. In *The Secret Diary of Adrian Mole* by Sue Townsend, Adrian includes an extract from his essay "My Thoughts on Scotland' in his entry for 30th August. Adrian is sure his writing is very impressive although even he admits, 'There are a couple too many "majestics"'.

"The hallowed mist rolls away leaving Scotland's majestic peaks revealed in all their majesty. A shape in the translucent sky reveals itself to be an eagle, that majestic bird of prey. Talons clawing, it lands on a loch, rippling the quiet majesty of the turbulent waters. The eagle pauses only to dip its majestic beak into the aqua before spreading its majestic wings and flying away to its magisterial nest high in the barren, arid, grassless hills.
The Highland cattle. Majestic horned beast of the glens lowers its brown-eyed shaggy-haired majestic head as it ruminates on the mysteries of Glencoe."

(a) Underline all the adjectives Adrian uses.

(b) Suggest adjectives he might have used instead of 'majestic'.

❑ In groups or pairs discuss which other adjectives Adrian has not chosen very wisely. Can you see where he contradicts himself? Imagine you are being asked to edit Adrian's contribution for the school magazine. Decide which adjectives you would omit altogether and which you would change. You may well decide one or two other changes in word choice are necessary also!

Comparison of Adjectives

Adjectives may be used to compare things.

    big   **bigger**   **biggest**

The simple adjective is called the **positive**;
The form for comparing two things is the **comparative**;
The form for comparing more than two is the **superlative**.

The comparative is usually formed by adding **r** or **er** to the positive and the superlative is formed by adding **st** or **est**:

| nice | **nicer** | **nicest** |
| cool | **cooler** | **coolest** |

Longer adjectives use '**more**' or '**most**' before the positive instead of these endings:

    exciting   **more exciting**   **most exciting**

A few forms are irregular:

    good   **better**   **best**

A few adjectives, because of their meaning, cannot be compared. Examples are: golden; left; fourth.

❑   You may have read the story of *Alice's Adventures in Wonderland*. At one point Alice eats a cake which makes her grow tall.

    "Curiouser and curiouser!" cried Alice (she was so much surprised, that for the moment she quite forgot how to speak good English); "now I'm opening out like the largest telescope that ever was!"

What would Alice have said if she *had* remembered how to speak good English?

Exercise 26

Copy this table, and fill in the comparative and superlative of the following adjectives :

Positive	Comparative	Superlative
1. large		
2. small		
3. flat		
4. tiny		
5. intelligent		
6. bad		
7. copper		

Did you spot the catch in one example?

O   O   O   O   O   O   O   O   O   O   O

memo:

When you are comparing two things only, use the comparative, not the superlative :

James is the **taller** of the twins.

Use the superlative when there are three or more things being compared.

James is the **tallest** in the class.

Exercise 27

Underline the correct degree of these adjectives :

1. The (larger / largest) of the two dogs was also the (fiercer / fiercest).
2. John is the (better / best) rugby player in the team.
3. Let us go to my house rather than yours as it is (nearer / nearest).
4. Both he and his wife have a car, but his is the (more / most) powerful.
5. Shep was the (more / most) reliable dog the farmer had ever had.

Buy the best!

In addition to comparing things directly, writers use comparative and superlative forms to convey a tone of enthusiasm. They are used extensively in the language of advertising :

"Dazzle washes <u>whiter</u>!"

"Large stocks of the <u>latest</u> machines at the <u>lowest</u> possible cost."

Exercise 28 (**More difficult** !)

In pairs or groups, look through the advertisements in a magazine and find two or more which use comparative and superlative forms in the written information. Cut out your advertisements, and circle all the examples of comparative and superlative adjectives that you find.

4.   ADVERBS

What does an adverb do?

Adverbs tell more about the verb. Some adverbs say more about adjectives or other adverbs.

'How' adverbs

Some adverbs tell 'how' something is done. These are sometimes known as 'adverbs of **manner**'. They are easy to recognise, as nearly all end in the letters -ly. Like adjectives, they help to create a vivid picture, but good writers usually use them sparingly.

truly	madly	deeply	quickly	despairingly
	joyfully	skilfully	sheepishly	neatly
	cleverly	stupidly		helplessly
	sweetly	bluntly	intently	artfully

'How' adverbs are formed by adding '-ly' to adjectives: quick / quickly.

Exercise 29

Form adjective / adverb pairs beginning with each of the letters of the alphabet. You may need a dictionary to help with some of the more unusual letters!

Exercise 30

(a)   Add 'how' adverbs to the following sentences. Try to choose an adverb which is interesting and adds significantly to the scene :

1.   The prisoner walked .... into the interview room.
2.   As he sat by the hospital bed, he watched the sick woman ....
3.   The boy's parents waited .... for the headmaster to speak.
4.   She looked .... at the stranger standing on the doorstep.
5.   He took up the letter .... and began to read it.

(b)   Swap your answers to (a) with members of another group. In your groups assess the answers the others have chosen. Discuss how the scenario in each example had been interpreted, and then decide which adverb contributed most effectively.

Exercise 31

A common fault of style is the use of redundant adverbs, that is, ones which contribute nothing of value to the meaning. Look at the 'how' adverbs in the following sentences. Decide which contribute something significant to the sentence. Then compare your results with a partner. Be prepared to explain why you have decided the adverb should be kept, or why it could be omitted without loss.

	Yes	No
1. Her mother broke down and cried <u>bitterly</u> at the news.		
2. He smiled <u>bitterly</u> at the memory of his schooldays.		
3. The children were playing <u>happily</u> in the garden.		
4. The dog gazed <u>hungrily</u> at the meat.		
5. The drowning man clutched <u>desperately</u> at the lifebelt.		
6. At the party he looked <u>desperately</u> for a familiar face.		
7. She blushed <u>shyly</u> at the compliment.		
8. She blushed <u>delightedly</u> at the compliment.		
9. The pupils fidgeted as the teacher's voice droned on <u>monotonously</u>.		
10. He laughed <u>uneasily</u> at the suggestion that he had been afraid.		

When ? - Where ?- How Much?

There are three other types of adverb which are a little more difficult to identify.

0 0 0 0 0 0 0 0 0 0 0

memo:

❑ *Adverbs of place tell* **where**. Put it <u>there</u>.

❑ *Adverbs of time tell* **when**. I shall stop <u>soon</u>.

❑ *Adverbs of degree tell* **how much**. I <u>quite</u> liked him.

Exercise 32

Say which type of adverb is used in the following sentences. The adverb is underlined for you. Then compare your answers with your partner's.

	How	When	Where	How Much
1. I shall talk to her <u>later</u>.				
2. The fisherman <u>nearly</u> caught a fish.				
3. We can meet <u>here</u>.				
4. He scowled <u>fiercely</u>.				
5. I posted the letter <u>yesterday</u>.				

5.   PRONOUNS

What is a pronoun?

A pronoun takes the place of a noun. Pronouns are used to avoid repeating nouns.

Horace was hiding from Susie but Susie has found Horace.

becomes

Horace was hiding from Susie but <u>she</u> has found <u>him</u>.

Personal Pronouns

'She' and 'him' are examples of **personal** pronouns which are used in place of nouns. Strange as it may seem, even if the meaning becomes less clear, it is still not usually considered good style in English to repeat a noun, and good writers make the meaning clear from the **context**, i.e., the situation in which the sentence occurs.

Look at this example :

> Ann said Ann would come.

It sounds clumsy and unnatural, and so we change the second 'Ann' to a pronoun :

> Ann said <u>she</u> would come.

❑   What two meanings could the above sentence have when the pronoun 'she' is substituted?

Exercise 33

(a)   Rewrite these sentences, using personal pronouns where necessary to avoid repeating the nouns.

1.   Asad told Asad's father that Asad would not be in for tea.
2.   The passengers said that the crew had done all the crew could to save the passengers.
3.   Miss Jenkins asked Lee where Lee's book was.
4.   Michael told Jim that Jim's wife had telephoned.
5.   The burglar shouted to the policeman not to move or the burglar would shoot.

(b)   With your partner or group, discuss which sentences would now require further clues to make the meaning clear.

Where is the pronoun?

Personal pronouns are rarely essential to meaning and they are often omitted in the abbreviated forms of English used in postcards, diaries, etc.

Wish you were here!

This famous traditional postcard greeting would read "**I** wish you were here" if it was written in full.

Exercise 34

Working in groups or pairs, write the full versions of these postcard and diary entries, adding all missing pronouns. (You will also sometimes need to add simple verbs such as 'is', 'was' and 'will' which are similarly omitted.)

O O O O O O O O

Monday 15th

Went to school. Last lesson Maths with Miss Stuart. Very boring. Met Steven at 3.30. Went to Macdonalds. Very busy so left quite soon.

*Jennifer and I arrived in
Venice this morning.
Really hot here. Went in a
gondola! The gondolier was
really young and good-
looking. Didn't sing to us,
though!! Saw St Marks
Square and bought some
presents. See you soon!*

Miss J Smith,

24, High Street,

Glasgow

Relative pronouns

who   which   what   that

So-called **relative pronouns** are used to provide a link between two sentences containing the same noun. This will be explained fully in Part Two of this book.

6.   CONJUNCTIONS

This road sign marks a **junction**: a joining of two roads. In the word conjunction, 'con' means 'together' so the whole word means 'joining together'.

It can be useful to remember that a conjunction is a **'joining word'**.

and	but	or	till	because
	although	since	if	unless
as	while	before	after	that
	though	than	when	until	so

Conjunctions can join together single words, phrases, clauses, or whole sentences. Sometimes the conjunction itself may be a phrase:

so that; in order to.

Writers may use conjunctions to achieve particular effects of style.

❑ Using more than one '**and**' in a list, for example, stresses the number and variety of the things:

"There were apples and pears and plums and apricots."

❑ Omitting conjunctions where they might be expected may create a tense, dramatic effect.

"I came, I saw, I conquered."

Conjunctions and Meaning

'**And**' is the conjunction which provides the simplest link.

However, other conjunctions can also give useful information on how the bits of language to be joined relate to each other. For example, '**but**' indicates a change or contrast, whereas '**if**' brings in a condition, '**because**' or '**since**' introduce a reason and so on.

You can often do better than 'and'

Exercise 35

In the following sentences the conjunction 'and' has been used as a link each time. Can you suggest alternatives which would bring out the meaning more effectively? You may rearrange the order if you wish, or put the conjunction at the beginning of the sentence instead of in the middle.

1. The explorer was wearing a thick padded suit <u>and</u> he was still cold.
2. He wanted to buy a leather jacket <u>and</u> he didn't have enough money.
3. The bank manager frowned <u>and</u> he began to speak.
4. James didn't know the number <u>and</u> he had to ring up Directory Enquiries.
5. I lived in Germany for two years <u>and</u> my German is quite good.
6. The house went on fire <u>and</u> I was inside.
7. The dog began to bark <u>and</u> the burglar ran away.
8. Her sister came in <u>and</u> Saima suddenly stopped talking
9. He was a nice man <u>and</u> he became a teacher.
10. He was small <u>and</u> he was strong.

Now compare your answers with a partner's. Add up the number of sentences in which you had thought of a *different* solution.

Exercise 36

This extract is adapted from *A Christmas Carol* by Charles Dickens.

When Scrooge awoke it was so dark, that he could scarcely distinguish the transparent window from the opaque walls of his chamber. He was endeavouring to pierce the darkness with his ferret eyes, when the chimes of a neighbouring church struck the four quarters. So he listened for the hour. To his great astonishment the heavy bell went on from six to seven, and from seven to eight, and regularly up to twelve; then stopped.

Twelve! It was past two when he went to bed. The clock was wrong. He scrambled out of bed, and groped his way to the window. He was obliged to rub the frost off with the sleeve of his dressing-gown before he could see anything; and could see very little then.

Scrooge went to bed again, and thought, and thought, and thought it over and over, and could make nothing of it. Scrooge lay in this state until the chime had gone three quarters more, when he remembered that the Ghost had warned him of a visitation when the bell tolled One. He resolved to lie awake until the hour was passed.

The hour bell sounded with a deep, dull, hollow, melancholy ONE. The curtains of his bed were drawn aside by a hand, and Scrooge found himself face to face with the unearthly visitor who drew them. It was a strange figure. But the strangest thing about it was, that from the crown of its head there sprung a bright, clear jet of light.

(a)   Pick out 6 different conjunctions used by Dickens in this piece of writing.

(b) ***Group Work***

In your groups discuss the following questions. One person should write down your conclusions :

1.   In sentence 4, (To his great astonishment ...), the author uses three conjunctions to link the phrases. What is the effect of using a number of conjunctions like this?

2.   Can you find another sentence in which conjunctions are repeated effectively within a short space?

Later on in this book you will learn how to use conjunctions to join up sentences.

7.   PREPOSITIONS

Roughly speaking, prepositions show the **position** of one thing in relation to another .

Horace is **on** the television.

Horace is **beside** the television.

Most prepositions are short, simple words.

above	across	after	among
at	with	beside	by
for	from	in	off
of	between	on	over
past	to	into	under

Exercise 37

Help Calum catch ten prepositions and put them in his basket.

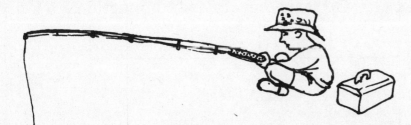

I was standing at the mouth of the River Oich which flows past my door, and I was gazing across Loch Ness. Suddenly my attention was drawn to a strange object that seemed to shoot out of the calm waters opposite the boathouse. A swan-like neck reached six feet or so above the water at its highest point, and the body, dark grey and glistening with moisture, was at least thirty feet long.

Which preposition should I use?

There are customs about which prepositions are used after particular adjectives and verbs.

For example, you compare your watch *with* someone else's, but you rely *on* the station clock.

0 0 0 0 0 0 0 0

memo:

❑ *Different **from** is correct in standard English. (Different **t o** is generally considered bad style; different **than** is correct only in American English.)*

❑ ***Between** is used with two; **among** with more than two.*

Exercise 38

Try this exercise in pairs, using a dictionary if necessary, to fill in the correct prepositions. (In some cases, more than one preposition is acceptable.) Saying the sentence out loud may help you to decide which preposition is correct.

1. The prisoner was convicted .... murder and sentenced .... death
2. Try to arrive .... time, please.
3. The money was shared .... Asif and Andy.
4. Emily Bronte suffered .... consumption and died .... the disease.
5. I am not satisfied .... your excuse.
6. The player was angry .... the referee's decision.
7. Black is the opposite .... white.
8. Although we are twins, my brother is different .... me in every way.
9. The orchard was separated .... the garden .... a wall.
10. According to the rules, you may not interfere .... an opponent's shot.

8.   ARTICLES

0   0   0   0   0   0   0   0   0   0   0

memo:

❑   The **definite article:** 'the' indicates a particular thing, or something previously mentioned. It is used with both singular and plural nouns.

❑   The **indefinite article:** 'a' or 'an' (before a vowel) indicates something that is not particular or has not been previously mentioned. It is singular only. In the plural it is either omitted, or a pronoun like 'some' may be used.

Exercise 39

With a partner or group, discuss the following pairs of sentences. Decide (i) if there is any difference between the two sentences. Then decide (ii) what the difference is and (iii) if the difference is big or small.

1.   *(a)*   "We can go into the castle," I said. "I have a key."
     (b)   "We can go into the castle," I said. "I have the key."

2.   *(a)*   I have the feeling that he is dishonest.
     (b)   I have a feeling that he is dishonest.

3.   *(a)*   Do you have an answer to the problem?
     (b)   Do you have the answer to the problem?

4.   *(a)*   Give me the book.
     (b)   Give me a book.

5.   *(a)*   Is the dark-haired man the Italian?
     (b)   Is the dark-haired man an Italian?

ST GEORGE'S SCHOOL FOR GIRLS

– ENGLISH DEPT –

Where is the 'the'?

Writers may omit articles in particular situations :

(a)   Newspaper Headlines :

(b)   Postcards and diaries:

> *Enjoying sights! Food excellent!*

Remember that personal pronouns and simple verbs are also often omitted in this style of English.

Exercise 40

Write out the complete versions, adding articles and any other words which are necessary in standard English.

1.   Rise in Price of Oil.
2.   Enjoying company and views of lake.
3.   Arrived on 4th. Job going well. Boss friendly.
4.   New Ship to be Built on Clyde.
5.   Queen Down Coal Mine.

Progress Report

So far, we have studied

❑   four types of **nouns**: **common**, **Proper**, **abstract** and **collective**.

❑   three tenses of **verbs**: **present**, **future** and **past**; three special parts of the **verb**: **infinitives** and **present** and **past participles**; how a verb has a **stem**, and may also have a **prefix** or **suffix**.

❑   **adjectives**, and how they may be used in comparisons.

❑   **adverbs**, which tell **how**, **when**, **where** and **how much**.

❑   how we use **pronouns**, **conjunctions**, **prepositions** and **articles**.

Section 2 : How words are spelt

Vowels and Consonants

The 26 letters of the alphabet are divided into two groups :

Vowels: a e i o u

Consonants: all the other letters.

The letter 'y' sometimes performs as a vowel, when it is similar in sound to 'i'. All words in English contain either a vowel or 'y'.

Exercise 1

Write down all the consonants. How many have a different sound? Which consonants are not strictly necessary in English?

Does our spelling system make sense?

I take it you already know
Of tough and bough and cough and dough?
Others may stumble but not you,
On hiccough, thorough, laugh and through.
Well done! And now you wish, perhaps,
To learn of less familiar traps?

Beware of heard, a dreadful word
That looks like beard and sounds like bird,
And dead : It's said like bed not bead -
For goodness' sake don't call it 'deed'!
Watch out for neat and great and threat -
(They rhyme with suite and straight and debt).

A moth is not a moth in mother
Nor both in bother, broth in brother,
And here is not a match for there
Nor dear and fear for bear and pear,
And then there's does and rose and lose -
Just look them up - and goose and choose,
And cork and work and card and ward,
And font and front and word and sword,
And do and go and thwart and cart...
(Anon.)

Read this poem aloud.

Your own accent may not make 'heard' and 'bird' sound the same, but you will see that the same sound in English can be represented in many different ways, and the same letter may represent different sounds.

The poem really just considers vowel sounds, but consonants show almost as much variety.

Exercise 2

Pick out six words mentioned in the poem, and write them down as they are sounded. Then think of another word with the same sound which has this simple spelling, e.g.

tough   (tuff)   cuff

This exercise will show you that many simple words in English *are* written as they are sounded, but that there are also many exceptions. Spelling in English is said to be **conventional**, which means it has become the custom to spell words in a certain way.

One of the main reasons for this is that English has adopted words from many different languages and in many cases has adopted a method of spelling as well. For example, in words adopted from Greek, the sound 'f' is always represented by the letters 'ph' which represent the Greek letter φ (phi).

Exercise 3

Using a dictionary if necessary, write down ten words starting with or containing the group of letters 'ph', and explain what they mean.

Do spelling rules help?

Many complicated rules have been formulated to help with spelling, but sometimes the rules themselves are so complicated and hard to remember, or have so many exceptions, that you would be quicker consulting a dictionary!

However, some rules are simple and helpful. Here are seven which should help to make things clearer. Some are in the form of a jingle, which makes them easier to remember. After each rule, there is an explanation and an exercise for practice.

RULE 1

'i' before 'e'
except after 'c'.

In words with the group of letters 'ie', where the sound is like 'ee' in 'feet', the 'i' always comes before the 'e' unless the 'ie' comes immediately after the letter 'c'.

❑   EXCEPTIONS: seize; weir; weird; protein.

Exercise 4

Tom is working at filling up the shelves. Can you help him put all the 'ie' words together, and all the 'ei' words together on the right shelves?

bel......ve ; conc......t; p......ce; c......ling; rec......pt; f......rce; y......ld; rec......ve; br......f; sh......ld; s......ge; s......ze; dec......tful; rel......f; perc......ve; w......rd; shr......k; repr......ve; conc......ve; ch......f.

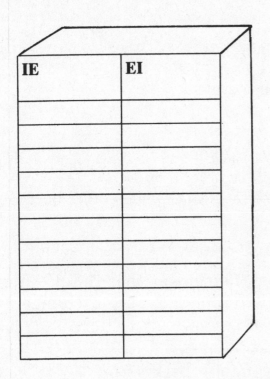

Exchange your book with a partner and check your answers. Add up your total out of 20.

RULE 2

For words ending in 'y' change 'y' to 'i' when the 'y' follows a consonant.

When adding suffixes to words ending in 'y', if the letter before the 'y' is a consonant, change the 'y' to 'i' before adding the suffix. If the letter before the 'y' is a vowel, keep the 'y' and add the suffix.

❑   EXCEPTION: adding **'ing'**. 'Y' is never changed to 'i' when 'ing' is added.

For example:

        fly + s   becomes   flies
                       but
        stay + s   becomes   stays.

        tidy + er   becomes   tidier
                       but
        fly + ing   becomes   flying

Exercise 5

Add endings to the following words. (Remember that the 'y' **doesn't** change after a vowel.) After completing each group, exchange your book with a partner's and check the answers.

1.   Add 's' to these words : try; guy; family; berry; ray.
2.   Add 'ed' to these words : marry; copy; supply; deny; obey.
3.   Add 'er' to these words : steady; pretty; easy; bust; heavy.
4.   Add 'ful' to these words : beauty; duty; pity; plenty; mercy.
5.   Add 'less' to these words : pity; mercy; penny.
6.   Add 'ly' to these words : angry; merry; easy; happy; busy.
7.   Add 'ment' to these words: merry; enjoy; employ; accompany.
8.   Add 'ness' to these words : lonely; lively; lovely; uneasy; empty; grey.
9.   Add 'age' to these words : marry; carry.
10.   Add 'ing' to these words : reply; journey; apply; copy; supply.

RULE 3

Disappearing 'e'

When a word ends with 'e', this letter is dropped when 'ing' or 'y' is added.

For example:

smoke .... smoking .... smoky

EXCEPTIONS

❑ Words ending in 'ie' change the 'ie' to 'y' when adding 'ing' :

tie - tying

❑ Words which would become identical to another word retain the 'e':

singe - singeing (not singing)
dye - dyeing (not dying)
hole - holey (not holy)

Exercise 6

1.   Add 'ing' to these words : lose; pause; arrange; prepare; create; deserve; dance; increase; become; tire.

2.   Add 'y' to these words : shade; ease; grime; noise; muscle; wire; slime; spine; flake; haze.

Exchange your book with a partner and check your answers. Add up your total out of 20.

RULE 4

Doubling final letters

When a word ends with ONE
vowel and ONE consonant,
this last letter is doubled
before a suffix.

For example: fat / fatter

BUT   lean / leaner

Exercise 7

Add these endings to the following words. (Remember, only double the
last letter if it is a **single** consonant following a **single** vowel):

1. Add 'ed' to these words: scrub; wrap; stop; knit; look.

2. Add 'er' to these words: run; join; work; sin; flat.

3. Add 'en' to these words: flat; mad; beat; red; bit.

4. Add 'est' to these words: big; dear; thin; sad; cool.

5. Add 'ing' to these words: flit; swim; lead; man; skip.

6. Add 'y' to these words: sun; fog; rain; fun; bag.

Exchange your book with a partner and check your answers. Add up
your total out of 30.

RULE 5

Double consonant follows
a short vowel;
Single consonant follows
a long vowel.

Before a suffix, double consonants are used when the vowel before them is **short**; a single consonant is used when the vowel before it is **long**. The letters 'c' and 'k' are not doubled, but 'ck' is used.

For example:

The deck chair cover was <u>striped</u>.

The traitor was <u>stripped</u> of his medal.

Read aloud the following tables of words to get an idea of what a 'short' or 'long' vowel is:

Short vowels	Long vowels
a as in pat	a as in fate
e as in bed	ee as in feet
i as in pit	i as in like
o as in pop	o as in vote
u as in pup	oo as in soot

EXCEPTION: The letter 'x' is not doubled after a short vowel: fixing; taxing.

MY MOST HATTED SUBJECT IS MATHS.

Exercise 8

Pick the right word out of the brackets.

1. (a)   The dressmaker was ------------ up the hem.
    (b)   The exile was -------------- for home.

                                          (pining/pinning)

2. (a)   I was --------- to win the prize.
    (b)   A robin came --------- onto the window sill.

                                          (hoping/hopping)

3. (a)   The cook --------- a cake for the wedding.
    (b)   He --------- an outsider to win the Derby.

                                          (baked/backed)

4. (a)   The typist sat --------- at her keyboard all morning.
    (b)   I am ---------- the programme on my video.

                                          (taping/tapping)

5. (a)   A --------- beggar limped through the rain.
    (b)   The Prince --------- when he did not get his way.

                                          (raged/ragged)

Exchange your book with a partner and check your answers. Add up
your total out of 10.

RULE 6

Single 'l'.

When joined to other words, 'all', 'will', 'full', 'skill', 'fill', and 'well' lose one 'l'.

WORDS TO LEARN

also	although	already	skilful	welfare
always	alone	fulfil	wilful	welcome

EXCEPTIONS: In American English, 'will' and 'skill' keep both 'l's.

Exercise 9

Look at the above table of words for five minutes, then cover them up. Your teacher will now dictate them to you. Write them correctly, remembering the 'single l' rule. Exchange your book with a partner and check your answers. Add up your total out of 10.

Is 'alright' all right?

As we have noted elsewhere in this book, our language is constantly changing. The form 'alright' is being used more and more frequently, although it is not yet officially recognised by all dictionaries. Collins dictionary gives it as an alternative spelling, but with the following warning :

> "The form *alright*, though very commonly encountered, is still considered by many careful users of English to be wrong or less acceptable than *all right*."

Our advice is to avoid using it until the dictionaries give it their full approval.

Exercise 10

When 'full' is added to a word to make an adjective, the final 'l' is dropped, as you would expect according to rule 6.

Form adjectives ending in 'ful' from the following words. Remember also to apply rule 2 for the words ending in 'y'.

spite	mercy	harm	use
plenty	care	joy	help
awe	thought	respect	skill

Exchange your book with a partner and check your answers. Add up your total out of 12.

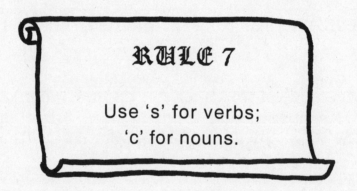

RULE 7

Use 's' for verbs;
'c' for nouns.

In the group of words which are otherwise identical in noun and verb forms, the verb is spelt with an 's' and the noun with a 'c'.

Learn the following examples :

NOUN	*VERB*
licence	license
practice	practise
advice	advise

Exercise 11

Decide whether you need a verb or a noun in the following examples, and fill in the correct form.

1.   Did the gunman have a licence / license for the weapon?
2.   My sister has to practice / practise her gymnastics exercises every day.
3.   The best advise / advice is often the hardest to accept.
4.   The motorist was prosecuted as he had forgotten to licence / license his car.
5.   Practice / practise makes perfect.
6.   I would advise / advice you to learn the spelling rules carefully.

Exchange your book with a partner and check your answers. Add up your total out of 6.

Progress Report

So far , you have now learned,

❑   Letters are either **vowels** or **consonants**.

❑   Spelling in English is **conventional**, so sounds are represented in many different ways.

❑   Seven rules to help you with your spelling.

Section 3 : How words are formed

Letters of the Alphabet

The smallest unit in a word is the letter. As we mentioned in the last chapter, the 26 letters are divided into two groups, vowels and consonants

❑   What do you notice about the words facetious and abstemious?

Syllables

The next unit in size within a word is the syllable. A syllable is a single separate sound - a beat, if you like. A word with three syllables would have three beats, e.g.

un - der - stand

Some words contain only one syllable. These are called monosyllables. These are the simplest and commonest words. Words with more than two syllables are called polysyllables.

A writer may use a number of monosyllables together to achieve a particular effect. The following lines are from a poem by Alfred Lord Tennyson, *The Lady of Shalott*. At this point, the spell under which the lady has been living has been broken, and this will lead to her death. What effect do you think the poet is aiming for here?

She left the web, she left the loom,
She made three paces through the room.

Exercise 1

Break up these words into syllables as was done with 'understand' on the previous page. Then put the number of syllables in brackets after each word.

case; family; jumping; impatient; happy; conditionally; intelligent; picture; intending; disappointment.

Compare your answers with a partner's. Did you always agree on the number of syllables? This can depend on your own pronunciation. If you disagree, then check the words with a good dictionary.

It is useful to be able to count the syllables in words. Japanese haiku poems, for example, depend on counting syllables. Here is an example written by a pupil. Can you work out how many syllables each line is supposed to contain?

Sally is my friend
She is clever in the head.
I'm the opposite.

Exercise 2

Now try to write a Haiku of your own. You could also choose a person as the topic, or you might choose an animal or flower, a natural thing like a rainbow; or if you are feeling ambitious, an abstract topic like 'Love'.

Parts of words

Do you remember that when we looked at verbs, we looked briefly at the different parts of the word? Nouns, adjectives and adverbs can be analysed in the same way.

☐ The stem is the main part which gives the basic meaning.

To the stem may be added a letter or group of letters which give extra information. It may alter the meaning of the stem or it may indicate what part of speech the whole word is. When the prefix or suffix is added, there may also be other small changes to the spelling of the stem.

☐ A prefix is added in front of the stem.

☐ A suffix follows the stem.

Word families (1)

Look at these 'family trees' of words.

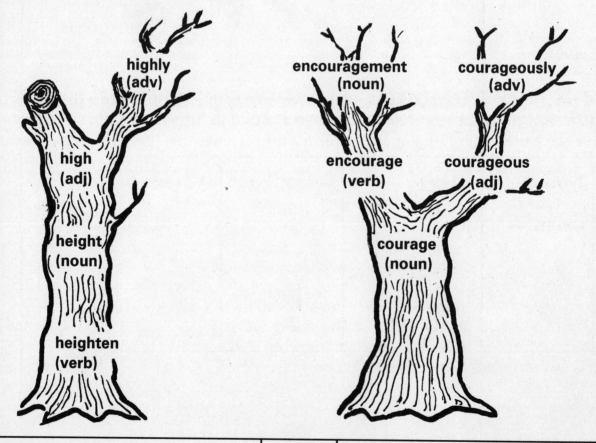

You will see that a suffix or prefix has been added to the stem word each time to form another word which is a different part of speech. A further prefix can sometimes be added, like a twig on a branch, to form yet another new word. Because the stem word remains the same, the words are all closely related in meaning.

Exercise 3

Make family trees of your own beginning with two or more of these stems. Put the part of speech formed in brackets :

   bright; glory; enjoy; terrible; attract; poor; obey.

(You can place the 'branches' of your trees wherever you like.)

Exercise 4

Make up some more word 'trees' of your own. It does not matter if you cannot form each one of the four parts.

Exercise 5

Make a table of the prefixes and suffixes which you used to form the different parts of speech. One or two are put in for you.

Noun	Verb	Adjective	Adverb
-ment	-en		

Word families (2)

Look at the following diagram.

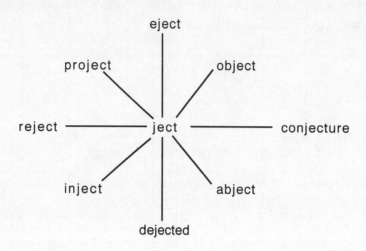

You will notice that each word contains the stem 'ject'. This stem comes from a Latin word which means 'to cast' or 'to throw'. This is known as the **root** of the word.

The prefixes, which also have Latin roots, tell more about the meaning. Here are twelve common prefixes derived from Latin:

de - down	ab - away	trans - across
re - back	sub - under	post - after
in (or im) - in	pre - before	circum - around
e or ex - out	pro - in front	con (or com) - together

❑   Can you now explain the meanings of 'rejected' and 'eject'?

Sometimes, the meaning of the English word remains very close to the root; but other times it changes. However it is often useful to notice the similarity of words as it may give you a clue to the meaning of a word you do not know.

❑   Look up the meaning of 'conjecture' in the dictionary. Can you suggest how the meaning relates to that of the root word?

❑   Can you think of another 'ject' word which is often used in school?

ST GEORGES SCHOOL
FOR GIRLS

ENGLISH DEPT

Exercise 6

Think of as many words as you can containing the following two stems and form diagrams similar to the one before. Use prefixes and suffixes to form your new words.

press; script

Masculine and Feminine

In grammar, words which refer to males are said to be **masculine**, and words which refer to females are termed **feminine**.

In English, the suffix 'ess' is often used to change masculine to feminine. for example :

lion   /   lioness

Exercise 7

(a)   Write down the feminine forms of : clerk; tiger; giant.

(b)   Now try three more difficult : duke; master; marquis.

(c)   With your partner, see how many more similar pairs you can think of.

'Not' prefixes

Some of the commonest prefixes in English are ones which mean 'not' and which create a word of opposite meaning when placed in front of the stem.

For example,   in   +   visible   gives us   invisible

ST GEORGE'S SCHOOL
FOR GIRLS

– ENGLISH DEPT –

Exercise 8

Pick out the correct prefix from below to form the opposite of each of the words in the following list:

regular; interesting; legal; understand; possible; legible; frequent; inflammable; normal; agree; pure; likely ; correct; trust.

in   im   un   mis   dis   ab   ir   non   il

A magpie language

The roots of the words you used in Exercise 6 came from one source language only, Latin. English has adopted words from many other languages also.

English is a very adaptable language, and over the centuries words have been 'borrowed' from the peoples with whom we have had contact. An 'etymological' dictionary is one which will tell you the origins of words. This information is usually in brackets at the very end of the entry.

Exercise 9

In pairs, look up the following words in an etymological dictionary. Write down the meaning and the source language of the word. You should be able to find 33 different source languages!

sky; house; nature; cycle; perfume; ballast; plunder; deck; piano; patio; shamrock; bog; mammoth; robot; algebra; yoghurt; shampoo; koala; tea; bamboo; skunk; anorak; canoe; amen; tattoo; catamaran; sherbet; cocoa; kiwi; junk (meaning a boat); zebra; pong; tycoon.

Native or Foreign?

English has its origins in a Germanic language which is referred to by the name Old English. At a very early stage, many words were added from the languages of the Vikings.

Following the Norman conquest, French words were adopted. Many words of Latin and Greek origin were introduced at the time of the Renaissance, and words from a wide variety of other languages were added during the time of the British Empire.

Of course, when something new is invented, a word must be invented to name it. The word 'television' was invented from a Greek root, 'tele' meaning 'at a distance' and a Latin root, 'vision' meaning to see.

It is useful to be able to comment on the choice of vocabulary an author uses, but it is not necessary to know 33 languages in order to do so. In general, our simplest and commonest words are derived from the ancient Old English and Scandinavian roots.

Longer, more intellectual words, which may give more precision of meaning, are derived from Latin, Greek and French. Authors use native English words when they are writing simply or informally. Formal, learned writing often makes use of more Classical roots.

Exercise 10

Without looking up a dictionary, say which word from these pairs you think is native English, and which is from a Classical language.

bad / disgusting   friend / acquaintance   good / excellent

new / novel   far / distant   speech / oration

speed / acceleration   talk / converse   sad / depressed

food / nourishment   body / physique.

Discuss

❑   Which of the two words you are more likely to use.

❑   Which is more likely to be used in speech and which in writing.

❑   In what circumstances might you prefer to choose the non-native word?

Progress Report

So far, we have learned,

❑   Words are composed of **letters** and **syllables**.

❑   Words have a **stem** and may also have a **prefix** or **suffix**.

❑   Prefixes and suffixes may alter the part of speech of the stem or may change its meaning.

❑   The origin of a word is its **root**. Modern English words have their roots in Old English and many other languages.

Part Two
How Groups of Words are Built Up

Section 1: What is a sentence?

A sentence is a group of words which make sense standing on their own. Sentences are the basic building bricks of language. Letters, stories, newspaper articles ... they are all made up of collections of sentences.

If a group of words is a sentence, there will be three things that we can say about it:

A sentence begins with a **capital letter** and ends with a **full stop**.

A sentence has a **subject** [the person or thing doing the action described in the sentence].

A sentence usually contains a complete form of a **verb**.

running down the street

This is NOT a sentence. 'Running' is only part of a verb (a present participle). There is no subject - we don't know who is running.

I was running down the street

This IS a sentence, as 'was running' is the whole past tense of the verb 'to run' and 'I' is the subject, the person doing the running. This is a complete statement, making sense on its own - in other words, a SENTENCE.

0   0   0   0   0   0   0   0   0   0   0

memo:

When you do the exercises which follow, remember that a sentence usually contains a subject and a complete form of the verb, and that it is a statement that makes sense standing on its own. A sentence might therefore be only two words long! 'I ran' is a complete sentence.

Exercise 1

Working in pairs, look at the following groups of words and discuss with your partner which ones are sentences and which ones are not. When you have decided, sort them out into the appropriate vans.

| During the holidays |
| In the house |
| They listened to the music |
| Listening to the music |
| When the meeting was over |
| The meeting was over |
| He is asleep |
| Feeling unwell |
| Susan felt unwell |
| The doctor said |
| I will send for the doctor |
| To the hospital |

Incomplete statements

Complete sentences

Exercise 2

Rewrite each of the following, putting in capital letters and full stops where required.

Always remember that *a sentence is a complete statement*. One way to test whether you have put your full stop in the right place is to ask yourself:

> If I were reading this aloud, where would I pause?

You would pause when you had finished a comment and this is where the full stop should go.

Watch out! One of these examples is a complete sentence already. Some of the examples should be split up into **two** sentences and some should be split up into **three**.

1. I would like a Ferrari my brother would prefer a Porsche
2. I took the car to the garage to have it repaired the mechanic didn't know what was wrong with it
3. When I'm seventeen I would like a car of my own my father said he wouldn't buy me one I could always buy a motorbike instead
4. I was too late for the bus yesterday this meant that I had to walk all the way to school
5. After the flood the roads were blocked
6. The dog ran out onto the road this could have caused an accident
7. Drivers think cyclists are a menace on the roads cyclists think drivers don't give them enough room

0   0   0   0   0   0   0   0   0   0   0

memo:

You may have found numbers 4 and 6 difficult, as a common mistake is to put a comma before the word 'this' when there should be a full stop. This error is sometimes called the 'comma splice'. Look out for it in the next exercise.

Exercise 3

David's teacher set the class a homework essay. The title was 'Our Journey'. Unfortunately, David forgot all about it and had to write it in a hurry on his way to school. He wrote it so quickly that he missed out all the punctuation. Rewrite the first page of his essay and help him get a better mark!

22 May

Our Journey
There was a traffic jam on the motorway it stretched for miles it took us three hours to reach the airport this left us feeling exhausted
Worse was to come just as we approached the airport a truck drove across the road in front of us this really gave my mother a fright she skidded into the ditch
We had to do something quickly or we would miss the plane .....

Exercise 4

Composition Work:

Write an essay continuing the story. Use David's last sentence as the first sentence of your own essay. Alternatively, write an essay describing *your* experiences on a journey. Whichever one you choose, take care with full stops!

Exercise 5

You may have heard of Penelope Lively's novel *The Ghost of Thomas Kempe*. It tells the story of a boy called James Harrison whose family moved into a very old house in Oxfordshire.

James started to dig up possessions belonging to a previous owner, Thomas Kempe, who had been a sorcerer - a kind of magician - in the seventeenth century. All kinds of unexpected happenings followed, as Thomas started to disturb James' family, sending him messages and getting him into all kinds of trouble.

Look for the book in your school or class library. Meanwhile, here are three extracts. Maybe the ghost has been at work here, because someone has removed most of the punctuation! Rewrite the passages correctly:

(a)   He was too busy during the rest of the day to think much more about the problem it was true about the measles there were only half the usual number of children in school this created a faintly holiday atmosphere the teachers were amiable and indulgent. *(There should be five sentences).*

(b)   He raced downstairs on the landing he slowed up he remembered the need for discretion, he crept down the next flight and tiptoed into the larder, he could hear his mother and Helen talking in the kitchen from overhead came sawing and hammering noises made by Bert, he felt scared. *(There should be seven sentences. Note that some of the commas should actually be full stops. You must decide which statements are complete sentences and change the commas to full stops if necessary.)*

(c)   The door opened, it banged itself shut again, twice, the windows rattled as though assaulted by a sudden thunderstorm, the calendar above the bed reared up, twitched itself from the hook and flapped to the floor, a glass of water on the bedside table tipped over and broke, it made a large puddle on the mat, downstairs James could hear the sitting-room door open, his father's footsteps plodded across the hall. (*There should be eight sentences. Again, some of the commas should be full stops.*)

Section 2: How sentences are made up

Another way to look at a sentence is to divide it into subject and predicate. The subject is the person or thing doing the action of the verb in the sentence. The rest of the sentence - no matter how long or short it is - tells us about the subject and is called the predicate. The predicate will include a verb and usually some other words too.

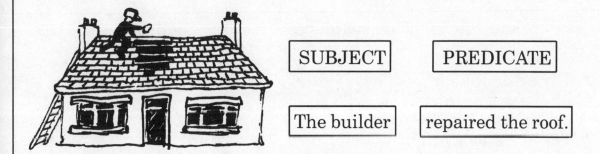

SUBJECT	PREDICATE
The builder	repaired the roof.

Exercise 1

The pile of bricks on the left hand side has to be built up into a wall of sentences containing subjects and predicates.

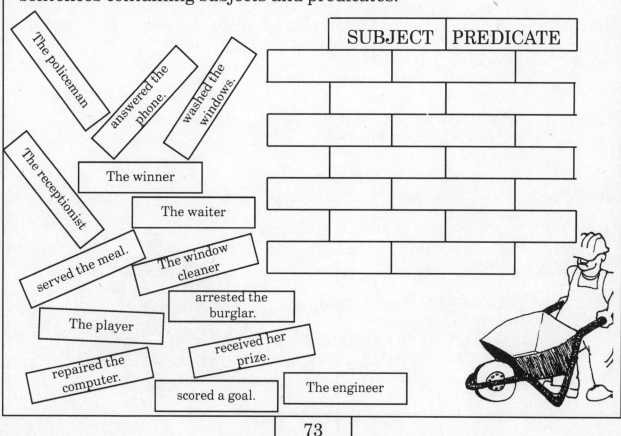

The policeman

answered the phone.

washed the windows.

The receptionist

The winner

The waiter

served the meal.

The window cleaner

arrested the burglar.

The player

received her prize.

repaired the computer.

scored a goal.

The engineer

SUBJECT	PREDICATE

O O O O O O O O O O

memo:

To find the subject in a sentence, pick out the verb, and then ask the question 'Who / what did this?'

Exercise 2

In pairs, look at the following sentences. First, pick out the verb. Then ask the question 'who' or 'what' to find the subject.

1. The bride wore a veil.
2. I have two sisters.
3. My brother is a doctor.
4. The sun shone brightly.
5. The janitor grudgingly retrieved the ball from the roof.

Where is the subject?

In English, the subject usually comes first, but not always. Look at the following examples. The subjects are marked in italics.

> *Grammar* is fun!
> Up shot *the flames*.
> *Superman* saved the world again.
> In July *we* go on holiday.

Exercise 3

Pick out the verbs and then the subjects of the following sentences, just as you did in Exercise 1.

1. By the stream sat a fisherman.
2. Into the room he strode.
3. Nicola was brushing her hair.
4. In April the Easter holidays begin.
5. Round her neck she wore a gold chain.

More difficult!

Look carefully at these two sentences:

> Come here!
> Run to the shops for me, please.

There appear to be no subjects. To find the subject, ask *who* is to come, *who* is to run to the shops. In such cases the subject is actually 'you', although it is not expressed. 'You' is said to be 'understood'.

Look at how the following sentences could be divided into subject and predicate.

> The girls played hockey.
> Every Saturday I visit my grandmother.
> Keep quiet!

First pick out the verbs. They are 'played', 'visit' and 'keep'. Find the subjects in the way you have been shown and enter them in the Subject column. Put the rest of the sentence (including the verb) into the Predicate column.

Subject	Predicate
The girls	played hockey
I	visit my grandmother every Saturday
(You)	Keep quiet

Exercise 4

Make up a table like the one above and then, working in pairs, divide up these sentences into subject and predicate.

1. In the fish tank Hussam found a shark.
2. Jack Sprat likes fat.
3. Yesterday we had games.
4. This is my last warning.
5. In the sand lay a diamond ring.
6. Close the door quietly.

The Object

Look at the following sentences:

>Susie opened the tin.
>My mother invited her friends to the house.

As you know, by putting the question 'Who' in front of the verbs, you can find the subject:

>*Who* opened the tin? The answer is 'Susie' and so 'Susie' is the subject.

>*Who* invited her friends to the house? The answer is 'My mother', and so 'My mother' is the subject.

Now put the questions 'what' or 'whom' *after* the verb:

>Susie opened what? . . . the tin.

>My mother invited whom? . . . her friends.

The answer to these questions is called the **object** of the sentence. Like the verb, the object is always part of the predicate. Any other part of the predicate (explaining where, when or how) is often called the extension. If you were asked to divide sentences up to show the parts of the predicate you could set them out like this:

Subject	Predicate		
	Verb	*Object*	*Extension*
Susie	opened	the tin.	
My mother	invited	her friends	to the house.

Exercise 5

Make up a table like the one on the previous page and divide these sentences into Subject and Predicate, showing verb, object and extension.

1. I drank a can of cola at break.
2. Mrs. White washes her clothes on Mondays.
3. The plumber repaired the faulty tap.
4. She hid the parcel under a cushion.
5. Christopher kicked the ball through the window.
6. Fiona read the part of Juliet in the play.
7. Every day she takes three pills.
8. He bathed his tired and aching feet.
9. I pasted some foreign stamps into my album.

Two Kinds of Object

You should now be able to identify the object in any sentence which has one in the predicate. But there are in fact two kinds of object.

Look at this sentence:

> Gordon gave his rabbit a carrot.

Use the test shown above: Gordon gave what? The answer is not 'his rabbit' but 'a carrot'. So 'a carrot' is the object. This is also called the **direct object**.

The carrot is given to the rabbit and this is said to be the **indirect object**. It answers the question 'To whom?' or 'To what?'

The actual thing given is called the	The person to whom it is given is called the
direct object	***indirect object***

We could show the make-up of this sentence in the form of a diagram which uses all the new words that have been introduced to you so far in Section 2: How sentences are made up.

Subject	Predicate		
Gordon	gave	his rabbit	a carrot
	VERB	INDIRECT OBJECT	DIRECT OBJECT

Exercise 6

Anne has started a new job as a school secretary. The first task she has to carry out is to pin up some notices. Help Anne sort out the direct and indirect objects which will complete the partly finished sentences already on the noticeboard. (Note: not all of the sentences contain two objects!)

SENIOR SCHOOL NOTICES

| Indirect Object | Direct Object |

1. THE MATHS TEACHER HAS GIVEN
2. THE HEADTEACHER SENT
3. THE RUGBY CAPTAIN SCORED
4. THE JANITOR SWEPT
5. THE SECRETARY LENT

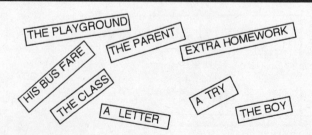

THE PLAYGROUND
HIS BUS FARE
THE PARENT
EXTRA HOMEWORK
THE CLASS
A LETTER
A TRY
THE BOY

Progress Report

So far, we have studied

❑   what makes a group of words a **sentence**.

❑   how a sentence can be divided into **subject** and **predicate**.

❑   how the predicate often contains an **object**.

❑   how there are two types of object: **direct** and **indirect**.

Section 3: Phrases and clauses

While the sentence is the main type of word group, there are two other important ones: **phrases** and **clauses**. These can be used in a sentence to make it longer or more detailed.

Do you remember how in Part 1 (Types of Words) we studied *parts of speech*? On page 26 we saw how an *adjective* can be added to a noun to tell us more about it.

0 0 0 0 0 0 0 0 0 0 0

memo:

Throughout the rest of this section, keep in mind this key idea:

A group of words can do the same job in a sentence as a single word.

Look at this example:

The red-haired girl was standing in the playground.

Here the word 'red-haired' describes the noun 'girl'. It is therefore an adjective.

We could turn the sentence round so that it reads:

The girl with red hair was standing in the playground.

What job do the words 'with red hair' do? They do the same job as the adjective 'red-haired' - they describe the girl. We have used a group of words to do the same job as a single adjective. We call a group of words like this an **adjective phrase**.

Exercise 1

The operation that you have to perform is to find and remove the adjective phrase from each of the following sentences. Follow this method:

FIRST: find the noun.

THIRD: you will see that these words begin with a preposition. (Look back to page 40 if you have forgotten what this word means!)

SECOND: find the words which describe the noun.

FOURTH: you have found the adjective phrase. Write it out.

1. The nurses at the hospital looked after the patients very well.
2. The house by the roadside was shaken by the passing traffic.
3. The athletes on the track had nearly reached the finishing line.
4. We bought a new video with a three-year guarantee.
5. The girl with long blonde hair used to be a model.

A clause is a group of words, like a phrase, but this time it also includes a **verb**.

In number 4 above, you will have noticed that the words 'with a three year guarantee' form an adjective phrase.

We could rewrite the sentence like this:

We bought a new video which came with a three year guarantee.

Here the words 'which came with a three year guarantee' are still doing the job of an adjective - that is, they describe or tell us more about the noun 'video'. But the difference is that this group of words also includes a verb ('came').

O O O O O O O O O O O

memo:

An adjective clause is a group of words containing a verb and doing the job of describing a noun.

Exercise 2

Collect in the supermarket trolley one adjective clause from each of the following sentences. Follow the same general four-step approach explained in the last exercise, but this time remember two other points:

The adjective clause will contain a verb.

The adjective *phrases* started with a preposition. The adjective *clauses* begin with a **relative pronoun**. (Look back to page 36 if you have forgotten about this!)

1. The checkout girl who was wearing a blue hairband looked very tired.
2. The chocolates which had been reduced sold out very quickly.
3. The window was covered with price stickers which the manager had put up.
4. The £1 coin which I placed in the slot released the trolley.
5. The checkout queue that I was standing in took a long time to move.
6. The supermarket where my sister works is always busy on Saturdays.

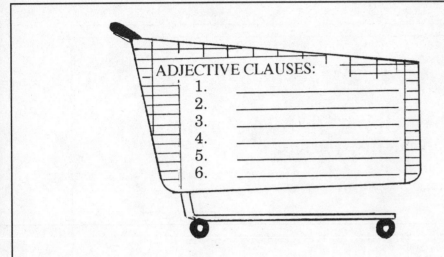

Exercise 3   **(More difficult!)**

Can you fit an adjective clause of your own into the goalposts in each of the sentences below? The first one has been done for you and you may find it useful to follow a similar pattern for the clauses that you make up yourself. Remember to check that each one contains a verb.

1. The goalkeeper **who was short-sighted** let the ball into the net.

2. The stadium ⌐‾‾‾‾‾⌐ had been built one hundred years ago.

3. The spectator ⌐‾‾‾‾‾⌐ could not find the right gate.

4. The football strip ⌐‾‾‾‾‾⌐ had to be returned to the shop.

Progress Report

So far, you have learnt that an adjective describing a noun can take the form of

❑   *a single word*

   e.g. <u>factory</u> workers [here 'factory' is an adjective as it describes 'workers']

❑   *a phrase*

   e.g. workers <u>in the factory</u> [an adjective phrase describing 'workers']

❑   *a clause*

   e.g. the workers <u>who worked in the factory</u> [an adjective clause containing a verb, describing 'workers']

Adverbial Phrases and Clauses

Just as adjective phrases and adjective clauses can do the same job as a single adjective, in the same way **adverbial phrases and clauses** can do the work of a single adverb.

Do you remember from pages 30-33 that adverbs usually tell us more about a verb? In the sentence 'The audience listened carefully to the new band' which word is an adverb?

Now look at this sentence.

I opened the drawer with great difficulty.

The words 'with great difficulty' tell us something about the verb 'opened' - they tell us HOW I opened the drawer. These words therefore do the work of an adverb. They are an **adverbial phrase**.

Exercise 4

Find the adverbial phrase in each of the following sentences.

o o o o o o o o o o

memo:

Remember that the adverbial phrase will tell you something more about the verb in the main part of the sentence, such as **how, why, when** *or* **where** *the action was done.*

1.   The sun rises in the east.
2.   The lion approached us with an angry roar.
3.   Carefully we made our way along the narrow path.
4.   The girl looked up with a puzzled expression.
5.   I was in school before nine o'clock.
6.   Snow has fallen on the hills.

1.	4.
2.	5.
3.	6.

An adverbial clause does the same job as an adverbial phrase, but just like an adjective clause it, too, contains a verb.

The sentence will therefore contain TWO verbs: the verb in the main part of the sentence, which the adverbial clause describes, plus another verb within the adverbial clause itself.

Puzzled? Then take a look at this example:

The spectators ran for cover when the rain came on.

There are two verbs here: 'ran' and 'came'. This means that the sentence contains two clauses.

The words 'when the rain came on' tell us something about the verb 'ran' - they tell us WHEN the spectators ran for cover. These words are therefore doing the job of an adverb. They are an **adverbial clause**.

Exercise 5

Write out the adverbial clause from each of the following sentences.

O   O   O   O   O   O   O   O   O   O   O

memo:

Remember that the adverbial clause will tell us more about the verb in the main part of the sentence.

1. My uncle stays with us whenever he is in Glasgow.
2. My trainers were found where I left them.
3. You are unlikely to pass your music exam unless you do more practice.
4. We could not play football because our ball was burst.
5. As I was running along the side of the swimming pool, I fell into the water.
6. Sarah won a gold medal because she was a good swimmer.
7. If you had turned up on time we could have had something to eat.
8. She was waiting on the platform when the train arrived.

1.	5.
2.	6.
3.	7.
4.	8.

You will notice that the adverbial clause can come at the start of the sentence or further on: its position does not matter. Its function remains the same: to tell us more about the verb in the main part of the sentence.

Exercise 6

Now add an adverbial clause of your own to each of the following sentences.

Remember that useful words to begin your adverbial clause are when, where, because, since, as, so that, if, although *. . . in other words, CONJUNCTIONS. As always, make sure that the words you add contain another verb. If they don't, then your 'clause' will not be a clause!*

1.   The bank robber hid the money (where. . .)
2.   I could not go to Kirsty's birthday party (because . . .)
3.   (. . .) he would not have sold the vase.
4.   The child would not stop crying (. . .)
5.   I did not know (. . .)

Principal and Subordinate Clauses

The clauses we have studied so far tell us more about the main part of the sentence. For this reason they are called **subordinate clauses**.

'Subordinate' means 'inferior to' or 'dependent on'. In the army a subordinate is an ordinary soldier who takes orders from an officer higher up, like a major or a general.

The subordinate clause, if you like, 'takes orders from' the main part of the sentence, which is called **the principal clause**. The principal clause could stand on its own as a sentence; the subordinate clause is a way of adding more information onto the principal clause. This brings us back to the point we started this section with: we can make a sentence longer by adding a phrase or clause to it.

Look at this sentence:

He found the treasure
where the pirates had
buried it.

The words 'He found the treasure'
make sense standing on their own as
a complete sentence. These words
are the **principal clause**.

The words 'where the pirates had buried it' could
not stand on their own; they are a **subordinate
clause**. As these words tell us more about the verb
found in the principal clause, they are a
subordinate adverbial clause.

Exercise 7

Divide these sentences into principal and subordinate clauses, and
decide whether the subordinate clauses are adjectival or adverbial.
The first one has been done for you on page 90.

1.   Julie, who is a fast runner, took part in the marathon.
2.   When I come home from school, I usually watch television.
3.   Goldfish never recognise their owners because they have a
      memory of only three seconds.
4.   My hamster, who is called Patch, needs a bigger cage.
5.   Although he is a pensioner, my neighbour enjoys computer
      games.
6.   If I can save up enough money, I will buy a new CD player.
7.   I will ask the teacher why she does not retire.

Principal Clause	*Subordinate Clause*	*Adverbial or Adjectival?*
1. Julie took part in the marathon	who is a fast runner	adjectival

Noun Clauses

Just as a clause can do the work of an adjective or adverb, it can also do the work of a noun.

Remember that in a simple sentence like
She ate a packet of crisps
we saw that the word she *is the subject and* packet of crisps *is the object?*

In the same way, in a sentence like

He decided that he would get married

the words 'that he would get married' do the same job as the object of the sentence. These words contain a complete verb ('would get') which means that they are a clause. As the words are doing the job of a noun, we have a **noun clause**.

Exercise 8

From each of the sentences, copy out the noun clause - that is, the group of words doing the work of a single noun as a subject or object in the sentence.

0   0   0   0   0   0   0   0   0   0

memo:

In each case the noun clause will answer the question 'what'? E.g. 'He decided that he would get married'. He decided 'what'? Answer: 'that he would get married'.

1.   The goalkeeper realised that the game was lost.
2.   'What you need is a bath!' exclaimed my mother.
3.   Do you think that you will tell them?
4.   What she told me was complete nonsense.
5.   That he had seen a ghost seemed quite unbelievable.

Progress Report

You now know that

❏   **a principal clause** can stand on its own as a sentence.

❏   **a subordinate adverbial clause** tells more about the action of the verb in the principal clause.

❏   **a subordinate adjective clause** describes a noun in the principal clause.

❏   **a noun clause** can do the job of a single noun as the subject or object of a sentence.

Section 4: How sentences are joined together

So far we have looked at how groups of words can be made up into sentences which can stand on their own. However, we often want to join sentences together to make longer ones.

*Do you remember that in Part One of this book we looked at **conjunctions, relative pronouns and participles?** Look back at pages 16-17 and 36 to remind yourself of these words. All three can be used to link sentences together.*

Conjunctions

A conjunction can come BETWEEN two sentences:

Saturday was a lovely day <u>but</u> we stayed indoors.

It can also come AT THE BEGINNING of the first sentence:

<u>Although</u> Saturday was a lovely day, we stayed indoors.

Exercise 1

Join each of the following groups of three sentences into a single sentence. Use one conjunction at the beginning and another in the middle.

1. The rain began to fall. We wanted to stop playing. The referee would not let us.
2. The ground was frozen. The game had to be cancelled. We still wanted to play.
3. Omar was very excited about the game. His father took him to the stadium. He usually went with his friends.

Exercise 2

Watch out! Sometimes people overuse the word 'so' as a conjunction, especially when writing a story. Rewrite these sentences, using an alternative conjunction to 'so'. Again, remember that you don't have to put the conjunction *between* the sentences; it can also go at the *beginning*.

1. It was pouring with rain so I stayed indoors.
2. I had forgotten to bring money with me so I couldn't buy a can of coke.
3. We missed the last bus so it was very late when we reached home.
4. I wanted a new computer game so I saved up my pocket money.

Relative Pronouns

Like the word 'conjunction', the word 'relative' has something to do with the idea of joining. Your relatives - aunts, uncles, etc. - are people you are 'joined' to by family ties.

You will remember that a pronoun is a word which can replace a noun (See Section 1, p. 33). A relative pronoun is a word which refers back to a noun AND joins the sentence to another one.

When we are talking about a *thing* we use the relative pronouns *which* or *that*:

> Stephen spends much of his spare time on his hobby. His hobby is building model aircraft.

These two sentences could be joined with a relative pronoun, as there is no need for the word 'hobby' to be used twice:

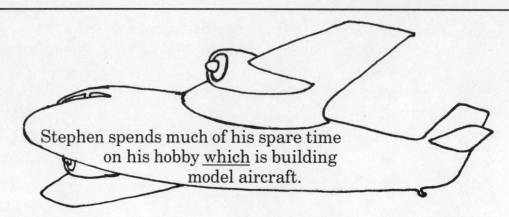

Stephen spends much of his spare time on his hobby <u>which</u> is building model aircraft.

When talking about people, we use the relative pronoun 'who':

Mr Beattie, <u>who</u> is a retired detective, lives next door.

0   0   0   0   0   0   0   0   0   0   0

memo:

The relative pronoun should always go beside the noun it relates to. Why would it not be right to say "The schoolbag was found by the P.E. teacher which had been left behind on the bus"?

Exercise 3

Join the following sentences together using the relative pronouns 'who' or 'which'. Remember that the relative pronoun always has to go beside the noun it relates to.

1. My friend bought a new computer. It is very useful for playing games.
2. I received a birthday card from my aunt in Canada. It contained some money.
3. A girl in our class was absent for four weeks. She has now returned to school.
4. The house has had new windows fitted. The house is next door to ours.
5. The bus was driving up the High Street. It almost knocked down the little boy.
6. Sarah is moving to a new school. Sarah is my best friend.
7. My younger brother told me a joke. It did not seem very funny.

8.   The field was empty. It was usually full of cattle.
9.   The sports centre is closed for repair. We go to the sports centre every Saturday.
10. The teacher handed out the exam papers. The teacher was new to the school.

Exercise 4

In these sentences the relative pronoun is in the wrong place. Rewrite them correctly.

1.   The boy fell off a ladder who broke his leg.
2.   The bride arrived at the church who was going to be married.
3.   The wedding was cancelled at short notice which was meant to take place at four o'clock.
4.   On the kitchen floor my dog made muddy footprints which had just been cleaned.

Participles

Do you remember that some parts of verbs are called past and present participles? The present participle is a form of the verb ending in 'ing' and the past participle usually ends in 'ed'.

You will find more information about participles on pages 16-17. As well as being used to form different verb tenses, participles can also be used as joining words.

   Neil was walking down the road. Neil slipped on a banana skin.

By missing out 'Neil was', the first sentence would become incomplete, and could therefore join on to the next one:

Walking down the road, Neil slipped on a banana skin.

Exercise 5

Join the following sentences using present participles. In some cases this will mean that you can miss out some of the words.

1.   Asim was sitting at the edge of the swimming pool. Asim dipped his toes in the water.
2.   Ian was driving his sports car down the motorway at 90 miles per hour. He was chased by a police car.
3.   David pulled with all his might. He managed to open the door which was jammed. [Hint: change one of the verbs into a present participle].
4.   John was waiting in the bus shelter. John could see the bus coming over the hill.
5.   The prisoner was creeping along the corridor. He managed to pass the guard without being seen.

These examples used **present participles** ending in 'ing'. **Past participles** (often ending in 'ed') can also be used as joining words.

I was tired by all the exercise. I fell asleep straight away.

These sentences could be joined as follows:

Tired by all the exercise, I fell asleep straight away.

Again, by missing out the words 'I was', the first sentence becomes an incomplete statement and can therefore be followed by a comma instead of a full stop.

Exercise 6

Join the following sentences using past participles.

1. The army was defeated by the enemy. The army made a hasty retreat.
2. The house was damaged beyond repair. It had to be demolished.
3. The team was depressed by all its defeats. It decided to give up playing in the league.

Joining sentences by a variety of methods

The separate exercises in this section have shown you how to join sentences using conjunctions, relative pronouns and participles. In an extended piece of written work, however, you should try to use all of these methods, so that you can achieve variety of sentence structure.

One of the things that can make a story very boring to read is when the writer keeps using the same sentence structures all the time. Aim for variety and your writing will become more lively and interesting.

Exercise 7

Join these sentences together using all of the methods you have learnt. Try to use as many different methods as possible in each exercise.

1. It was a bright summer's morning. We decided to go for a walk on the hills. We put on hiking boots. We set out before everyone else was awake. An hour later we reached the summit. From there we were able to look down on the village. It was lying before us. The mist came down suddenly. We decided that it was time to go back down. We saw a bus approaching. We managed to get a ride home. We were exhausted.

2.   Tyson had left him. There was silence. It was more complete silence than Peter had ever known. It seemed as though the eighteen feet of soil above his head was pressing down. It was silent. He was able to hear the faint hiss of air through the pipe. This pipe was coming along the upper tunnel. The pipe came down the shaft. It came along the wall of the lower tunnel. This was his connection with the outside world. He took the knife. He began to hack away at the clay in front of him.

Section 5: Building sentences into paragraphs

In the 1930s a joiner in Denmark called Kirk Christiansen was nearly bankrupt. He persuaded his nine brothers to lend him enough money to start a small factory making wooden toys. Later, Christiansen came up with the idea of making plastic building bricks: Lego.

It took more than 35,000,000 Lego bricks to build all the houses, palaces and cathedrals in the Legoland theme park in Denmark!

Sentences are the basic 'building bricks' of language and - like Lego bricks - they can interlock to produce bigger units. We call these units paragraphs.

O O O O O O O O O O

memo:

A paragraph is a collection of sentences which are all to do with the same subject. Start a new paragraph when you are changing to a new topic, or a different aspect of a topic.
The first line should be indented slightly.

Exercise 1

The following sentences are taken from a tourist leaflet about the town of Aberfoyle, but they are not in the right order.

Build them into a proper paragraph by writing them on to the bricks on the wall shown on the following page.

When you have finished you should have an interlocking series of sentences with each one following on from the one before it.

Fortunately more peaceful times lay ahead.

In the mists of history, Aberfoyle was associated with Celtic princes.

His novel *Rob Roy* ensured the fame of the Trossachs and brought visitors flocking to Aberfoyle.

However, by the sixteenth century, King James VI had to summon local landowners and instruct them to impose order.

Later the surrounding area became home to wild clans like the Macgregors.

Today Aberfoyle is a peaceful town but it had a very turbulent past.

It was Sir Walter Scott who, in the nineteenth century, put Aberfoyle on the map as a tourist resort.

You may have started your paragraph with the sentence

Today Aberfoyle is a peaceful town but it had a very turbulent past.

This sentence is different from the others. Instead of mentioning a particular stage of Aberfoyle's history, it introduces a general idea which the rest of the paragraph develops in more detail. We call this kind of sentence a **topic sentence**.

The topic sentence is usually - but not always - the first sentence in the paragraph.

Look at the following paragraph carefully:

A wide range of outdoor pursuits are well suited to forest surroundings. These include rambling, canoeing, horseriding, birdwatching, hill climbing and fishing. In addition to this, arrangements for other specialist activities like orienteering or clay pigeon shooting may be made between a club and the Forester in charge. However, the vast majority of people come to the forest simply to picnic and to walk.

Look how each 'building brick' interlocks with the next one to produce a well-organised paragraph:

> The first sentence is a **topic sentence**, telling the reader what the paragraph is going to talk about.

> The second sentence develops the first point by giving a list of examples.

> The third sentence adds on a similar point, using the linking phrase in addition to this.

> The last sentence makes a slightly different point, using the word however to provide a link back to the previous point.

Exercise 2

Construct a paragraph of your own using a similar pattern. Begin with this topic sentence:

> There are many difficulties which young teenagers have to face in the world today.

Develop this topic sentence into a paragraph of about six to eight lines, by providing examples and presenting the sentences in a logical order so that one point leads on to the next.

Here are a few other useful linking words and phrases which can be used at the start of a new sentence:

Adding on similar points	*Making points different from the previous one*	*Drawing a conclusion*
Furthermore		As a result of
In the same way	Nevertheless	Therefore
Similarly	On the other hand	Consequently
	In contrast	Thus

Of course, all paragraphs do not follow exactly the same pattern. If they did, many essays, newspaper articles or books would be very dull and repetitive! It is, however, useful to know how to organise your thoughts in this way.

Section 6 : How words are separated

Once upon a time there were three bears daddy bear mummy bear and baby bear they lived together in a cottage in a dark wood every morning they would have a bowl of porridge for breakfast daddy bear had a great big bowl mummy bear had a middle-sized bowl and baby bear had a . . .

Punctuation marks

When we talk, we pause for breath, and when we read, we also need to pause from time to time to understand what we are reading. Punctuation marks provide these pauses, and they also form a kind of code, giving hints to the meaning.

Stops: full stops; exclamation marks; question marks.

❑   These are all used to indicate that a sentence has ended. They also give the added information that the sentence is a **statement**, a **question** or an **exclamation**.

❑   All of these stops are followed by a **capital** letter.

Horace is behind the television.

Where is the goldfish?

How hungry my goldfish is today!

Exercise 1

Put a full stop, exclamation mark or question mark after each of the following sentences.

1. How happy Horace is looking
2. Susie loves her cat
3. When did Columbus discover America
4. Susie won a goldfish at the fair
5. What luck
6. Why did Alice grow taller suddenly

Pauses : commas, colons and semi-colons

❏   A comma shows a pause in a sentence. It has also some special functions which you will be asked to work out in Exercise 2.

❏   A colon (:) is generally an 'introducing' pause: it points forward to a quotation, an explanation or a more detailed description to follow.

❏   A semi-colon (;) is generally a 'finishing' pause: it marks the end of a sentence but less firmly than a full stop does. It often comes between two statements which contrast or are closely connected.

❏   The use of colons and semi-colons varies from one writer to another, but if you use them yourself as explained above you will not go wrong. The semi-colon is particularly useful: if you master it, you can avoid the 'comma splice' mistake described on page 69 which is so common.

❏   'Pausing' punctuation marks are followed by a **small** letter.

Exercise 2

Look at the following examples with your partner. Decide what special job the comma or commas is doing in each one.

1.   There were swans, ducks, geese and water-hens on the lake.
2.   Come here at once, Jim!
3.   "I shall see you at six," he said.
4.   The yacht, gleaming white in the sun, lay at anchor in the bay.

Don't underestimate the comma! It can sometimes greatly alter the meaning of a sentence.

Exercise 3

Look at these sentences with your partner or group. Can you work out what each sentence would mean without the commas?

1.   The man, he knew, was a crook.
2.   Do you have a sister, Valerie?
3.   The spectators, I saw, were bored.
4.   This is my uncle, Stephen.
5.   Mother, Teresa is at the door.

Exercise 4

Write out the following sentences. Decide if the pause in each is an 'introducing' pause or a 'finishing' pause, and put in a colon or a semi-colon as required.

1.   Children generally like sweet flavours / adults on the whole prefer savoury.
2.   He explained to the estate agent what he wanted / a home by the sea, with four bedrooms and a large garden.
3.   There were three excellent features in the story / humour, suspense and a surprise ending.
4.   After an arduous journey we arrived at the hotel / a hot meal and a bath soon restored our spirits.
5.   The view was breath-taking / silver sands, waving palm trees and deep blue water.

Speech Marks

Speech marks (also called **quotation marks** or **inverted commas**) enclose the **actual words** used by a speaker. Usually, double commas are used, but single ones are used for 'speech within speech'.

This would be written as

"My goldfish has disappeared," said Susie.

❑   Punctuation marks belonging to the direct speech, such as question marks, exclamation marks and commas, go inside the speech marks.

❑   You will notice in the example that a full stop at the end of a sentence in the direct speech becomes a comma before a verb of speaking.

❑   Speech marks should never be seen back to back : " ". A new paragraph should be taken whenever you open speech marks.

❑   Speech marks are also used to enclose quotations, and in handwriting they may enclose titles, although italics are generally used for this in print. Usually, double inverted commas are used for quotations and single for titles, but there is no strict rule about this.